# THE SEARCH FOR THE
# TROJAN HORSE

by Myka-Lynne Sokoloff
illustrated by Bruce Emmett

Cover, ©Walter Bibikow/Index Stock; p.4, ©Bettmann/CORBIS; p.5, ©Araldo de Luca/CORBIS; p.6, ©Réunion des Musées Nationaux/Art Resource, NY; p.8-9, ©Musee des Beaux-Arts, Blois, France, Lauros/Giraudon/The Bridgeman Art Library; p.9, ©akg-images/Peter Connolly; p.10, ©Erich Lessing/ Art Resource, NY; p.11, ©Bildarchiv Preussischer Kulturbesitz/Art Resource, NY; p.12, ©Wolfgang Kaehler/CORBIS; p.13, ©Scala/Art Resource, NY.

Printed in China

ISBN 10: 0-15-377388-X
ISBN 13: 978-0-15-377388-4

Ordering Options
ISBN 10:  0-15-377149-6 (Grade 5 Collection)
ISBN 13:  978-0-15-377149-1 (Grade 5 Collection)
ISBN 10:  0-15-377866-0 (package of 5)
ISBN 13:  978-0-15-377866-7 (package of 5)

2 3 4 5 6 7 8 9 10   0940   17 16 15 14 13 12 11 10 09

The best gift Heinrich Schliemann ever received was a book about world history. This book included tales of Greek and Roman history. One of the stories told was about the fall of the ancient city of Troy. That story quickly grabbed hold of Heinrich's imagination.

Heinrich was eight years old when he first encountered this story. He envisioned that he would find the remains of the city of Troy one day. In fact, Heinrich did grow up to become one of the most famous archeologists of all time. Most people think that he succeeded in finding Troy, the city of Greek legends.

It's hard to know where myth ends and history begins in Greece. Many people believe that ancient Greek stories are simply made up. Some scholars, however, think that the heroes and plots of these stories were based on real people and events.

Heinrich
Schliemann

Heinrich Schliemann was one of these scholars. The funny thing is you can't tell where history ends and myth begins in the life of Schliemann either! Some people think he made up many "facts" about his life. He was an interesting man, to be sure.

Heinrich Schliemann was born in New Buckow, Germany, on January 6, 1822. When Heinrich was a boy, he used to dig in the dirt with a girl named Minna. The children envisioned that they were archaeologists, digging for buried treasures from the past. They promised that when they grew up they would marry and hunt for real treasures around the world.

When Heinrich was fourteen years old, he first learned the stories of ancient Greece. He then worked on a small ship that took him across the sea. During his time at sea, Heinrich learned a lot about the world outside Germany. In addition, he was exposed to many new languages.

Soon Heinrich learned to read and write in many languages, including Dutch, English, German, Italian, Spanish, French, Russian, and Greek. He continued to travel around the world on business.

As he got older, Heinrich specialized in studying ancient languages. His childhood friend Minna had married someone else. Heinrich decided he wanted to marry a woman who could recite ancient Greek poems by heart. He soon met a woman named Sophia and was so taken with her that he wanted to marry her. Lucky for him, she felt the same way about him and agreed to marry him.

Heinrich put his own language skills to good use. He read many works by ancient Greek and Roman writers. One he could not put out of his mind— the story of the Trojan horse.

The poet Homer wrote tales about the Trojan War.

## The Ancient Tale

Troy was an ancient city in what is now northwest Turkey. The city is widely remembered as the home of the Trojan War. "Trojans" was the name given to the ancient residents of this particular city. The story behind the fall of Troy is long and complicated. Here is how it goes.

The setting is at the end of a ten-year war that probably took place around 1250 B.C. during a period known as the Bronze Age. In Greek mythology there is a story about two men, Menelaus and Paris, who fought each other. Menelaus was the king of ancient Greece. Paris was a young visitor from the city of Troy. Menelaus and Paris did not get along, and soon a terrible war broke out.

Menelaus (left), a king of Ancient Greece

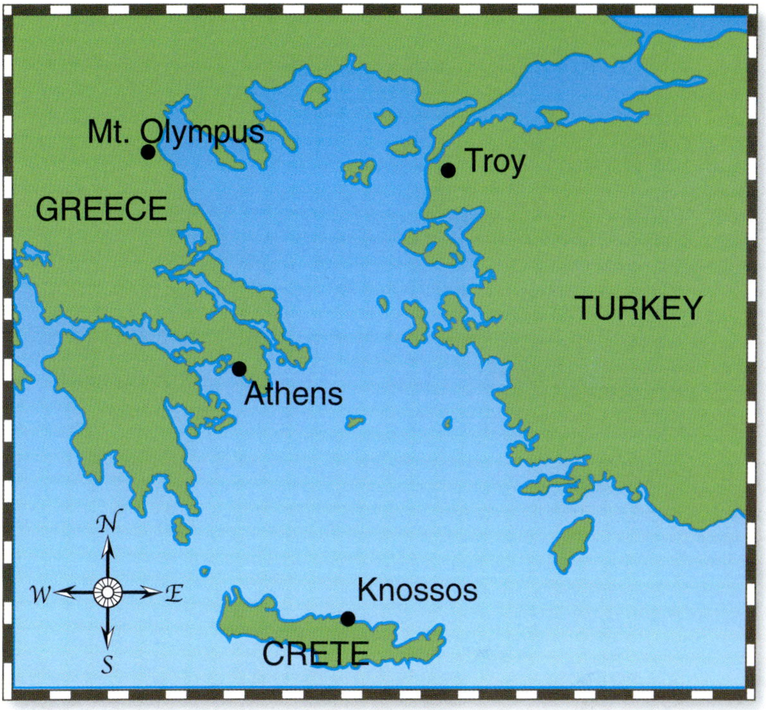
Mt. Olympus
Troy
GREECE
TURKEY
Athens
N
W
E
S
Knossos
CRETE

Preparing for war, Menelaus gathered soldiers from all over Greece. His brother, King Agamemnon, was the most powerful ruler in the world. He would lead the Greek armies and ships to Troy to fight Paris and the Trojans.

Battle raged between the Greeks and the Trojans for ten years below the hill city of Troy. Many famous Greek heroes and gods took part in the war. Zeus, the father of all gods, wanted the Trojans to win the war. Athena, goddess of war, sided with the Greeks.

As the Greeks got closer and closer to Troy, the Trojan people believed that they could resist the Greek army as long as a special wooden statue remained within the walls of their city. It was kept at the Temple of Athena. However, two Greek heroes managed to steal the statue. Once they captured the statue, the citizens of Troy felt they were no longer safe from attack by the Greeks.

The story goes that Athena told the Greeks to build a wooden horse of giant proportions. When the horse was finished, the finest Greek soldiers hid inside. The remaining Greeks burned their tents and returned to their ships. The ships soon sailed out of sight.

The next day, the Trojans saw that the Greeks had left. They figured the enemy had given up and gone home. They discovered the giant horse just outside the gates to their city, a mysterious gift left in the night.

The Trojans were quite curious about the giant horse. Was it a gesture of peace, or maybe a sign from the gods? They decided to move it inside the city gates.

Two wise people of Troy knew that the horse meant trouble. "Don't do it!" they warned. "Beware of Greeks bearing gifts!" The Trojans refused to listen. That was a huge mistake.

An ancient Greek helmet

The enormous horse would not fit through the city gates. Stone by stone, the Trojans began to tear down the walls around Troy so that they could get the horse through. Once the horse was inside the city, the Trojans began to celebrate their victory. They rejoiced a bit too soon, however.

A Greek soldier who had been left behind signaled the Greek ships to return to Troy once the horse was inside the wall. Then, under the cover of night, the Greek soldiers who had been hiding in the giant wooden horse climbed out. They surprised and attacked the Trojans.

King Menelaus found Paris inside the city. Then the Greeks conquered the Trojan people and burned the city to the ground.

Athena was watching all of these events unfold. She became angry when the Greeks stole the statue from her temple and burned it. Although Athena had helped the Greeks during most of the war, she now wanted to punish them.

As a result, the Greeks ran into all kinds of trouble on their way home. Some of the ships sank on the voyage. Others traveled for many years before they would reach home. Athena got her revenge, or so the story goes.

## FINDING TROY

Heinrich Schliemann had made lots of money in business. Therefore, he could follow his dream of finding Troy. He would piece together clues from his research to locate the city.

The amateur archaeologist began to dig in Turkey. He chose a spot that matched the description of Troy in ancient stories. Heinrich hired dozens of workers to help dig. Many people think Heinrich was sloppy in his work. As he dug, he destroyed many valuable clues about the city's history. At the time, though, this was how most archaeologists worked. Today archaeologists are much more careful.

Excavations of Troy

During Schliemann's archeological digs, he uncovered the ruins of many cities. Sometimes the ruins appeared in layers because a city was built and then destroyed only to be rebuilt again on the same ground. This resulted in digs that uncovered layers of ruins. He believed that one of the layers was the city of Troy. Many archaeologists believe that Schliemann was in the correct place. However, many disagree about which layer was the city of Troy.

## Schliemann at Mycenae

For a while, with no success, Heinrich Schliemann took a break from digging for Troy. He went to look for the palace of Agamemnon, the brother of Menelaus, in southern Greece. In 1876, Schliemann uncovered the ruins of an ancient kingdom in Mycenae. There he found many pieces of jewelry, art objects, and metal work. He also found the tombs where the rulers of Mycenae were buried. By studying these objects, archeologists have learned much about the city's rich history and daily life.

Schliemann found this mask at Mycenae in a tomb. He thought it showed the face of Agamemnon.

During Heinrich's digging, he had access to many ancient treasures. Some people claim that he incorrectly identified objects and where they came from, including the ones he considered to be from Troy. This led to a large amount of skepticism about Heinrich's work.

Other questions remain, too. Did the Trojan horse really exist? Were the Greek and Trojan heroes real people? Although pictures of the horse appeared in artwork in ancient times, no piece of the original horse has ever been found.

One thing is for sure, though. Like the heroes of ancient Troy, the stories about Heinrich Schliemann—myth or fact—will live on.

# Think Critically

1. Retell the main events of the Trojan War in order.

2. Why did the Greeks need to steal the special wooden statue from the Temple of Athena in Troy?

3. What is the author's main purpose in writing the section with the heading "Finding Troy"?

4. How does the Greeks' use of the Trojan horse go along with the theme of Common Goals?

5. Do you think the Trojan horse existed? Why or why not?

 **Social Studies**

**Make a Time Line** Create an illustrated time line of the sequence of events that unfolded around the Trojan horse in this book.

**School-Home Connection** Share the story of the Trojan horse with members of your family. Then discuss whether or not you think the story of the Trojan horse is true.

**Word Count:** 1,485 (with graphic 1,493)